Edmund Burke

A Letter from Mr. Burke, to a Member of the National Assembly

In Answer to Some Objections to His Book on French Affairs

Edmund Burke

A Letter from Mr. Burke, to a Member of the National Assembly
In Answer to Some Objections to His Book on French Affairs

ISBN/EAN: 9783337241636

Printed in Europe, USA, Canada, Australia, Japan

Cover: Foto ©Suzi / pixelio.de

More available books at **www.hansebooks.com**

A

LETTER

FROM

Mr. *BURKE,*

TO A

MEMBER OF THE NATIONAL
ASSEMBLY;

IN ANSWER TO

SOME OBJECTIONS TO HIS

BOOK ON FRENCH AFFAIRS.

———

THE SECOND EDITION.

———

PARIS, PRINTED,

AND LONDON RE-PRINTED FOR J. DODSLEY, PALL-MALL.

M.DCC.XCI.

SIR,

I HAD the honour to receive your letter of the 17th of November laſt, in which, with ſome exceptions, you are pleaſed to conſider favourably the letter I have written on the affairs of France. I ſhall ever accept any mark of approbation, attended with inſtruction, with more pleaſure than general and unqualified praiſes. The latter can ſerve only to flatter our vanity; the former, whilſt it encourages us to proceed, may help to improve us in our progreſs.

Some of the errors you point out to me in my printed letter are really ſuch. One only I find to be material. It is corrected in the edition which I take the liberty of ſending to you. As to the cavils which may be made on ſome part of my remarks, with regard to the *gradations* in your new conſtitution, you obſerve juſtly,

B   that

that they do not affect the substance of my objections. Whether there be a round more or
less in the ladder of reprefentation, by which your
workmen afcend from their parochial tyranny to
their federal anarchy, when the whole fcale is
false, appears to me of little or no importance.

I published my thoughts on that conftitution,
that my countrymen might be enabled to efti-
mate the wifdom of the plans which were held
out to their imitation. I conceived that the true
character of thofe plans would be beft collected
from the committee appointed to prepare them.
I thought that the fcheme of their building would
be better comprehended in the defign of the architects than in the execution of the mafons. It
was not worth my reader's while to occupy himfelf with the alterations by which bungling practice corrects abfurd theory. Such an inveftiga-
tion would be endlefs: becaufe every day's paft
experience of impracticability has driven, and
every day's future experience will drive, thofe
men to new devices as exceptionable as the old;
and which are no otherwife worthy of obferva-
tion than as they give a daily proof of the delu-
fion of their promifes, and the falfehood of their
profeffions. Had I followed all thefe changes,
my

my letter would have been only a gazette of their wanderings; a journal of their march from error to error, through a dry dreary defart, unguided by the lights of heaven, or by the contrivance which wifdom has invented to fupply their place.

I am unalterably perfuaded, that the attempt to opprefs, degrade, impoverifh, confifcate, and extinguifh the original gentlemen, and landed property of an whole nation, cannot be juftified under any form it may affume. I am fatisfied beyond a doubt, that the project of turning a great empire into a veftry, or into a collection of veftries, and of governing it in the fpirit of a parochial adminiftration, is fenfelefs and abfurd, in any mode, or with any qualifications. I can never be convinced, that the fcheme of placing the higheft powers of the ftate in churchwardens and conftables, and other fuch officers, guided by the prudence of litigious attornies and Jew brokers, and fet in action by fhamelefs women of the loweft condition, by keepers of hotels, taverns, and brothels, by pert apprentices, by clerks, fhop-boys, hair-dreffers, fidlers, and dancers on the ftage, (who, in fuch a commonwealth as your's, will in future overbear, as already they have overborne, the fober in-

B 2   capacity

capacity of dull uninſtructed men, of uſeful but la‑
borious occupations) can never be put into any
ſhape, that muſt not be both diſgraceful and
deſtructive. The whole of this project, even if
it were what it pretends to be, and was not in
reality the dominion, through that diſgraceful
medium, of half a dozen, or perhaps fewer, in‑
triguing politicians, is ſo mean, ſo low‑minded,
ſo ſtupid a contrivance, in point of wiſdom, as
well as ſo perfectly deteſtable for its wickedneſs,
that I muſt always conſider the correctives which
might make it in any degree practicable, to be
ſo many new objections to it.

In that wretched ſtate of things, ſome are
afraid that the authors of your miſeries may be
led to precipitate their further deſigns, by the
hints they may receive from the very arguments
uſed to expoſe the abſurdity of their ſyſtem, to
mark the incongruity of its parts, and its
inconſiſtency with their own principles; and
that your maſters may be led to render their
ſchemes more conſiſtent, by rendering them
more miſchievous. Excuſe the liberty which
your indulgence authoriſes me to take, when I
obſerve to you, that ſuch apprehenſions as theſe
would prevent all exertion of our faculties in
this great cauſe of mankind.

A raſh

A rafh recourfe to *force* is not to be juftified
in a ftate of real weaknefs. Such attempts bring
on difgrace; and, in their failure, difcounte-
nance and difcourage more rational endeavours.
But *reafon* is to be hazarded, though it may be
perverted by craft and fophiftry; for reafon can
fuffer no lofs nor fhame, nor can it impede any
ufeful plan of future policy. In the unavoidable
uncertainty, as to the effect, which attends on
every meafure of human prudence, nothing feems
a furer antidote to the poifon of fraud than its
detection. It is true the fraud may be fwallowed after this difcovery; and perhaps even
fwallowed the more greedily for being a detected
fraud. Men fometimes make a point of honour
not to be difabufed; and they had rather fall into
an hundred errors than confefs one. But after
all,—when neither our principles nor our difpofitions, nor, perhaps, our talents, enable us to
encounter delufion with delufion, we muft ufe
our beft reafon to thofe that ought to be reafon-
able creatures, and to take our chance for the
event. We cannot act on thefe anomalies in
the minds of men. I do not conceive that the
perfons who have contrived thefe things can
be made much the better or the worfe for
any thing which can be faid to them. *They*

are

are reafon proof. Here and there, fome men, who were at firft carried away by wild good intentions, may be led, when their firft fervors are abated, to join in a fober furvey of the fchemes into which they have been deluded. To thofe only (and I am forry to fay they are not likely to make a large defcription) we apply with any hope. I may fpeak it upon an affurance almoft approaching to abfolute know-ledge, that nothing has been done that has not been contrived from the beginning, even before the ftates had affembled. *Nulla nova mihi res inopinave furgit.* They are the fame men and the fame defigns that they were from the firft, though varied in their appearance. It was the very fame animal that at firft crawled about in the fhape of a caterpillar, that you now fee rife into the air, and expand his wings to the fun.

Proceeding, therefore, as we are obliged to proceed, that is upon an hypothefis that we addrefs rational men, can falfe political principles be more effectually expofed, than by demonftrating that they lead to confequences directly inconfiftent with and fubverfive of the arrangements ground-ed upon them ? If this kind of demonftration is not permitted, the procefs of reafoning called
deductio

deductio ad absurdum, which even the severity of geometry does not reject, could not be employed at all in legiflative difcuffions. One of our ftrongeft weapons againft folly acting with authority, would be loft.

You know, Sir, that even the virtuous efforts of you patriots to prevent the ruin of your country have had this very turn given to them. It has been faid here, and in France too, that the reigning ufurpers would not have carried their tyranny to fuch deftructive lengths, if they had not been ftimulated and provoked to it by the acrimony of your oppofition. There is a dilemma to which every oppofition to fuccefsful iniquity muft, in the nature of things, be liable. If you lie ftill, you are confidered as an accomplice in the meafures in which you filently acquiefce. If you refift, you are accufed of provoking irritable power to new exceffes. The conduct of a lofing party never appears right: at leaft it never can poffefs the only infallible criterion of wifdom to vulgar judgments—fuccefs.

The indulgence of a fort of undefined hope, an obfcure confidence, that fome lurking remains of virtue, fome degree of fhame, might exift in the breafts of the oppreffors of France, has been among the caufes which have helped to

bring

bring on the common ruin of king and people. There is no fafety for honeft men, but by believing all poffible evil of evil men, and by acting with promptitude, decifion, and fteadinefs on that belief. I well remember, at every epocha of this wonderful hiftory, in every fcene of this tragic bufinefs, that when your fophiftic ufurpers were laying down mifchievous principles, and even applying them in direct refolutions, it was the fafhion to fay, that they never intended to execute thofe declarations in their rigour. This made men cautious in their oppofition, and remifs in early precaution. By holding out this fallacious hope, the impoftors deluded fometimes one defcription of men, and fometimes another, fo that no means of refiftance were provided againft them, when they came to execute in cruelty what they had planned in fraud.

There are cafes in which a man would be afhamed not to have been impofed on. There is a confidence neceffary to human intercourfe, and without which men are often more injured by their own fufpicions than they could be by the perfidy of others. But when men, whom we *know* to be wicked, impofe upon us, we are fomething worfe than dupes. When we know them, their fair pretences become new motives

for

for diftruft. There is one cafe, indeed, in which it would be madnefs not to give the fulleft credit to the moft deceitful of men, that is, when they make declarations of hoftility againft us.

I find, that fome perfons entertain other hopes, which I confefs appear more fpecious than thofe by which at firft fo many were deluded and dif-armed. They flatter themfelves that the extreme mifery brought upon the people by their folly, will at laft open the eyes of the multitude, if not of their leaders. Much the contrary, I fear. As to the leaders in this fyftem of impofture,—you know, that cheats and deceivers never can repent. The fraudulent have no refource but in fraud. They have no other goods in their magazine. They have no virtue or wifdom in their minds, to which, in a difappointment concerning the pro-fitable effects of fraud and cunning, they can retreat. The wearing out of an old, ferves only to put them upon the invention of a new delu-fion. Unluckily too, the credulity of dupes is as inexhauftible as the invention of knaves. They never give people poffeffion; but they always keep them in hope. Your ftate doctors do not fo much as pretend that any good whatfoever has hitherto been derived from their operations, or that the public has profpered in any one inftance, under their management. The nation is fick,

very

very fick, by their medicines. But the *charlatan* tells them that what is paft cannot be helped;— they have taken the draught, and they muft wait its operation with patience ;—that the firft effects indeed are unpleafant, but that the very fick- nefs is a proof that the dofe is of no flug- gifh operation ;—that ficknefs is inevitable in all conftitutional revolutions ;—that the body muft pafs through pain to eafe ;—that the prefcriber is not an empirick who proceeds by vulgar expe- rience, but one who grounds his practice on * the fure rules of art, which cannot poffibly fail. You have read Sir, the laft Manifefto, or Moun- tebank's bill, of the National Affembly. You fee their prefumption in their promifes is not leffened by all their failures in the performance. Compare this laft addrefs of the Affembly, and the prefent ftate of your affairs with the early en- gagements of that body; engagements which, not content with declaring, they folemnly de- pofed upon oath, fwearing luftily that if they were fupported they would make their country glorious and happy ; and then judge whether thofe who can write fuch things, or thofe who can bear

* It is faid in the laft quackifh addrefs of the National Affembly to the people of France ; that they have not formed their arrangements upon vulgar practice ; but on a theory which cannot fail, or fomething to that effect.

to read them, are of *themfelves* to be brought to
any reasonable courfe of thought or action.

As to the people at large, when once thefe
miferable fheep have broken the fold, and have
got themfelves loofe, not from the reftraint, but
from the protection of all the principles of natural authority, and legitimate fubordination, they
became the natural prey of impoftors. When
they have once tafted of the flattery of knaves,
they can no longer endure reafon, which appears
to them only in the form of cenfure and reproach.
Great diftrefs has never hitherto taught, and
whilft the world lafts it never will teach, wife
leffons to any part of mankind. Men are as
much blinded by the extremes of mifery as by
the extremes of profperity. Defperate fituations
produce defperate councils, and defperate meafures. The people of France, almoft generally,
have been taught to look for other refources
than thofe which can be derived from order,
frugality, and induftry. They are generally
armed; and they are made to expect much
from the ufe of arms. *Nihil non arrogant armis.*
Befides this, the retrograde order of fociety has
fomething flattering to the difpofitions of mankind. The life of adventurers, gamefters, gip-
fies, beggars, and robbers, is not unpleafant.
It requires reftraint to keep men from falling
into

into that habit. The shifting tides of fear and hope, the flight and pursuit, the peril and escape, the alternate famine and feast, of the savage and the thief, after a time, render all course of slow, steady, progressive, unvaried occupation, and the prospect only of a limited mediocrity at the end of long labour, to the last degree tame, languid, and insipid, Those who have been once intoxicated with power, and have derived any kind of emolument from it, even though but for one year, never can willingly abandon it. They may be distressed in the midst of all their power; but they will never look to any thing but power for their relief. When did distress ever oblige a prince to abdicate his authority? And what effect will it have upon those who are made to believe themselves a people of princes?

The more active and stirring part of the lower orders having got government, and the distribution of plunder, into their hands, they will use its resources in each municipality to form a body of adherents. These rulers, and their adherents, will be strong enough to overpower the discontents of those who have not been able to assert their share of the spoil. The unfortunate adventurers in the cheating lottery of plunder will probably be the least sagacious, or the most inactive and irresolute of the gang.

If,

If, on difappointment, they fhould dare to ftir, they will foon be fuppreffed as rebels and mutineers by their brother rebels. Scantily fed for a while, with the offal of plunder, they will drop off by degrees; they will be driven out of fight, and out of thought; and they will be left to perifh obfcurely, like rats, in holes and corners.

From the forced repentance of invalid mutineers and difbanded thieves, you can hope for no refource. Government itfelf, which ought to conftrain the more bold and dextrous of thefe robbers, is their accomplice. Its arms, its treafures, its all, are in their hands. Judicature, which above all things fhould awe them, is their creature and their inftrument. Nothing feems to me to render your internal fituation more defperate than this one circumftance of the ftate of your judicature. Many days are not paft fince we have feen a fet of men brought forth by your rulers for a moft critical function. Your rulers brought forth a fet of men, fteaming from the fweat and drudgery, and all black with the fmoak and foot of the forge of confifcation and robbery—*ardentis maffæ fuligine lippos*, a fet of men brought forth from the trade of hammering arms of proof, offenfive and defenfive,

in

in aid of the enterprizes, and for the subsequent
protection of housebreakers, murderers, traitors,
and malefactors; men, who had their minds sea-
soned with theories perfectly conformable to their
practice, and who had always laughed at pof-
session and prescription, and defied all the
fundamental maxims of jurisprudence. To the
horror and stupefaction of all the honest part
of this nation, and indeed of all nations who
are spectators, we have seen, on the credit of
those very practices and principles, and to carry
them further into effect, these very men placed
on the sacred seat of justice in the capital city of
your late kingdom. We see, that in future,
you are to be destroyed with more form and regularity. This is not peace; it is only the in-
troduction of a sort of discipline in their hostility.
Their tyranny is complete, in their justice; and
their lanthorn is not half so dreadful as their
court.

One would think that out of common decency they would have given you men who had
not been in the habit of trampling upon law
and justice in the assembly, neutral men, or
men apparently neutral, for judges, who are to
dispose of your lives and fortunes.

Cromwell, when he attempted to legalize his
power, and to settle his conquered country in a

state

ſtate of order, did not look for his diſpenſers of juſtice in the inſtruments of his uſurpation. Quite the contrary. He ſought out with great ſollicitude and ſelection, and even from the party moſt oppoſite to his deſigns, men of weight, and decorum of character; men unſtained with the violence of the times, and with hands not fouled with confiſcation and ſacrilege : for he choſe an *Hales* for his chief juſtice, though he abſolutely refuſed to take his civic oaths, or to make any acknowledgment whatſoever of the legality of his government. Cromwell told this great lawyer, that ſince he did not approve his title, all he required of him was, to adminiſ- ter, in a manner agreeable to his pure ſentiments and unſpotted character, that juſtice without which human ſociety cannot ſubſiſt : that it was not his particular government, but civil order itſelf, which as a judge he wiſhed him to ſupport. Cromwell knew how to ſeparate the inſtitutions expedient to his uſurpation from the adminiſtra- tion of the public juſtice of his country. For Cromwell was a man in whom ambition had not wholly ſuppreſſed, but only ſuſpended the ſenti- ments of religion, and the love (as far it could conſiſt with his deſigns) of fair and honourable reputation. Accordingly, we are indebted to this act of his for the preſervation of our laws, which

which fome fenfelefs affertors of the rights of
men were then on the point of entirely erafing,
as relicks of feudality and barbarifm. Befides,
he gave in the appointment of that man, to that
age, and to all pofterity, the moft brilliant example of fincere and fervent piety, exact juftice,
and profound jurifprudence *. But thefe are not
the things in which your philofophic ufurpers
choofe to follow Cromwell.

One would think, that after an honeft and neceffary Revolution (if they had a mind that
theirs fhould pafs for fuch) your mafters would
have imitated the virtuous policy of thofe who
have been at the head of revolutions of that
glorious character. Burnet tells us, that nothing tended to reconcile the Englifh nation to
the government of King William fo much as
the care he took to fill the vacant bifhoprics
with men who had attracted the public efteem
by their learning, eloquence, and piety, and
above all, by their known moderation in the
ftate. With you, in your purifying Revolution, whom have you chofen to regulate the
church ? Mr. Mirabeau is a fine fpeaker—and
a fine writer,—and a fine—a very fine man;—
but really nothing gave more furprize to every

* See Burnet's life of Hales.

body

body here, than to find him the fupreme head
of your ecclefiaftical affairs. The reft is of courfe.
Your Affembly addreffes a manifefto to France
in which they tell the people, with an infulting
irony, that they have brought the church to its
primitive condition. In one refpect their de-
claration is undoubtedly true; for they have
brought it to a ftate of poverty and perfecution.
What can be hoped for after this ? Have not
men (if they deferve the name) under this new
hope and head of the church, been made bifhops, for no other merit than having acted as
inftruments of atheifts; for no other merit than
having thrown the children's bread to dogs; and
in order to gorge the whole gang of ufurers;
pedlars, and itinerant Jew-difcounters at the
corners of ftreets, ftarved the poor of their
Chriftian flocks, and their own brother paftors?
Have not fuch men been made bifhops to ad-
minifter in temples, in which (if the patriotic
donations have not already ftripped them of their
veffels) the churchwardens ought to take fecurity
for the altar plate, and not fo much as to truft
the chalice in their facrilegious hands, fo long as
Jews have affignats on ecclefiaftic plunder, to
exchange for the filver ftolen from churches?

C   I am

I am told, that the very fons of fuch Jew-jobbers have been made bifhops; perfons not to be fufpected of any fort of *Chriftian* fuperftition, fit colleagues to the holy prelate of Autun; and bred at the feet of that Gamaliel. We know who it was that drove the money-changers out of the temple. We fee too who it is that brings them in again. We have in London very refpectable perfons of the Jewifh nation, whom we will keep: but we have of the fame tribe others of a very different defcription,—houfebreakers, and receivers of ftolen goods, and forgers of paper currency, more than we can conveniently hang. Thefe we can fpare to France, to fill the new epifcopal thrones: men well verfed in fwearing; and who will fcruple no oath which the fertile genius of any of your reformers can devife.

In matters fo ridiculous, it is hard to be grave. On a view of their confequences it is almoft inhuman to treat them lightly. To what a ftate of favage, ftupid, fervile infenfibility muft your people be reduced, who can endure fuch proceedings in their church, their ftate, and their judicature, even for a moment! But the deluded people of France are like other madmen, who, to a miracle, bear hunger, and thirft, and

cold,

cold, and confinement, and the chains and lash of their keeper, whilst all the while they support themselves by the imagination that they are generals of armies, prophets, kings, and emperors. As to a change of mind in these men, who consider infamy as honour, degradation as preferment, bondage to low tyrants as liberty, and the practical scorn and contumely of their upstart masters, as marks of respect and homage, I look upon it as absolutely impracticable. These madmen, to be cured, must first, like other madmen, be subdued. The sound part of the community, which I believe to be large, but by no means the largest part, has been taken by surprize, and is disjointed, terrified, and disarmed. That sound part of the community must first be put into a better condition, before it can do any thing in the way of deliberation or persuasion. This must be an act of power, as well as of wisdom; of power, in the hands of firm, determined patriots, who can distinguish the misled from traitors, who will regulate the state (if such should be their fortune) with a discriminating, manly, and provident mercy; men who are purged of the surfeit and indigestion of systems, if ever they have been admitted into the habit of their minds; men who will lay the foundation of a real re-

form,

form, in effacing every veftige of that philofophy which pretends to have made difcoveries in
the *terra auftralis* of morality; men who will
fix the ftate upon thefe bafes of morals and politics, which are our old, and immemorial, and,
I hope, will be our eternal poffeffion.

This power, to fuch men, muft come from
without. It may be given to you in pity; for
furely no nation ever called fo pathetically on
the compaffion of all its neighbours. It may be
given by thofe neighbours on motives of fafety
to themfelves. Never fhall I think any country
in Europe to be fecure, whilft there is eftablifhed,
in the very centre of it, a ftate (if fo it may be
called) founded on principles of anarchy, and
which is, in reality, a college of armed fanatics,
for the propagation of the principles of affaf-
finaticn, robbery, rebellion, fraud, faction, op-
preffion, and impiety. *Mahomet*, hid, as for a time
he was, in the bottom of the fands of Arabia,
had his fpirit and character been difcovered,
would have been an object of precaution to provident minds. What if he had erected his fa-
natic ftandard for the deftruction of the Chriftian religion in *luce Afiæ*, in the midft of the then
noon-day fplendour of the then civilized world?
The princes of Europe, in the beginning of this
century, did well not to fuffer the monarchy of
France

France to fwallow up the others. They ought not now, in my opinion, to fuffer all the monarchies and commonwealths to be fwallowed up in the gulph of this polluted anarchy. They may be tolerably fafe at prefent, becaufe the comparative power of France for the prefent is little. But times and occafions make dangers. Inteftine troubles may arife in other countries. There is a power always on the watch, qualified and difpofed to profit of every conjuncture, to eftablifh its own principles and modes of mifchief, wherever it can hope for fuccefs. What mercy would thefe ufurpers have on other fovereigns, and on other nations, when they treat their own king with fuch unparalleled indignities, and fo cruelly opprefs their own countrymen?

The king of Pruffia, in concurrence with us, nobly interfered to fave Holland from confufion. The fame power, joined with the refcued Holland and with Great Britain, has put the emperor in the poffeffion of the Netherlands; and fecured, under that prince, from all arbitrary innovation, the antient, hereditary conftitution of thofe provinces. The chamber of Wetzlar has reftored the Bifhop of Leige, unjuftly difpoffeffed by the rebellion of his fubjects. The king

of

of ·Pruffia was bound by no treaty; nor. alliance of blood, nor had any particular reafons for thinking the emperor's government would. be more mifchievous or more oppreffive. to human- nature. than that of the Turk ; yet on mere. motives of policy that prince has interpofed with the threat of all his force; to fnatch even the Turk from the pounces of the imperial. eagle. ' If this is´done in favour of a. barbarous nation, with a barbarous neglect of police, fatal to the human race, in favour of a nation, by principle in eternal enmity with the Chriftian name; a nation which will not fo much as give the falutation of peace (Salam) to any. of us; nor make any pact with any Chriftian·nation beyond a truce ;—if. this be done in favour of the Turk, fhall it be thought either impolitic, or unjuft, or uncharitable, to employ the fame power, to refcue from captivity a virtuous·monarch (by. the courtefy of Europe confidered as Moft Chriftian) who, after an intermiffion of 175 years, had called together the ftates of his kingdom, to reform abufes, to eftablifh a free´government, and to ftrengthen his .throne; a monarch, who at the very outfet, without force, even without follicitation, had given to. his people fuch a

Magna

Magna Charta of privileges, as never was given by any king to any fubjects?—Is it to be tamely borne by kings who love their fubjects, or by fubjects who love their kings, that this monarch, in the midft of thefe gracious acts, was infolently and cruelly torn from his palace, by a gang of traitors and affaffins, and kept in clofe prifon to this very hour, whilft his royal name and facred character were ufed for the total ruin of thofe whom the laws had appointed him to protect?

The only offence of this unhappy monarch towards his people, was his attempt, under a monarchy, to give them a free conftitution. For this, by an example hitherto unheard of in the world, he has been depofed. It might well difgrace fovereigns to take part with a depofed tyrant. It would fuppofe in them a vitious fympathy. But not to make a common caufe with a juft prince, dethroned by traitors and rebels, who profcribe, plunder, confifcate, and in every way cruelly opprefs their fellow citizens, in my opinion is to forget what is due to the honour, and to the rights of all virtuous and legal government.

I think the king of France to be as much an object both of policy and compaffion as the

C 4   Grand

Grand Seignor or his ftates. I do not conceive, that the total annihilation of France (if that could be effected) is a defirable thing to Europe; or even to this its rival nation. Provident patriots did not think it good for Rome, that even Carthage fhould be quite deftroyed; and he was a wife Greek, wife for the general Grecian interefts, as well as a brave Lacedemonian enemy, and generous conqueror, who did not wifh, by the deftruction of Athens, to pluck out the other eye of Greece.

However, Sir, what I have here faid of the interference of foreign princes is only the opinion of a private individual; who is neither the reprefentative of any ftate, nor the organ of any party; but who thinks himfelf bound to exprefs his own fentiments with freedom and energy in a crifis of fuch importance to the whole human race.

I am not apprehenfive that in fpeaking freely on the fubject of the King and Queen of France, I fhall accelerate (as you fear) the execution of traiterous defigns againft them. You are of opinion, Sir, that the ufurpers may, and that they will, gladly lay hold of any pretext to throw off the very name of a king;—affuredly I do not wifh ill to your king; but better for him not to

live

live (he does not reign) than to live the paffive inftrument of tyranny and ufurpation.

I certainly meant to fhew, to the beft of my power, that the exiftence of fuch an exe- cutive officer, in fuch a fyftem of republic as theirs, is abfurd in the higheft degree. · But in demonftrating this—to *them*, at leaft, I can have made no difcovery. They only held out· the royal name to catch thofe Frenchmen to whom the name of king is ftill venerable. They calcu- late the duration of that fentiment; and when they find it nearly expiring, they will not trouble themfelves with excufes for extinguifhing the name, as they have the thing. They ufed it as a fort of navel-ftring to nourifh their unnatural offspring from the bowels of royalty itfelf. Now that the monfter can purvey for its own fubfift- ence, it will only carry the mark about it, as a token of its having torn the womb it came from. Tyrants feldom want pretexts. Fraud is the ready minifter of injuftice; and whilft the currency of falfe pretence and fophiftic reafoning was expedient to their defigns, they were under no neceffity of drawing upon me to furnifh them with that coin. But pretexts and fophifms have had their day; and have done their work. The

ufurpation

ufurpation no longer feeks plaufibility. It trufts
to power.

Nothing that I can fay, or that you can fay,
will haften them by a fingle hour, in the execution of a defign which they have long fince entertained. In fpite of their folemn declarations,
their foothing addreffes, and the multiplied oaths
which they have taken, and forced others to
take, they will affaffinate the king when his name
will no longer be neceffary to their defigns; but
not a moment fooner. They will probably firft
affaffinate the queen, whenever the renewed
menace of fuch an affaffination lofes its effect
upon the anxious mind of an affectionate hufband.
At prefent, the advantage which they derive
from the daily threats againft her life, is her only
fecurity for preferving it. They keep their fovereign alive for the purpofe of exhibiting him,
like fome wild beaft at a fair; as if they had a
Bajazet in a cage. They choofe to make monarchy contemptible by expofing it to derifion, in the
perfon of the moft benevolent of their kings.

In my opinion, their infolence appears more
odious even than their crimes. The horrors of
the 5th and 6th of October were lefs deteftable
than the feftival of the 14th of July. There are
fituations

fituations (God forbid I fhould think that of the
5th and 6th of October one of them) in which the
beft men may be confounded with the worft, and
in the darknefs and confufion, in the prefs and
medley of fuch extremities, it may not be fo
eafy to difcriminate the one from the other.
The neceffities created, even by ill defigns, have
their excufe. They may be forgotten by others,
when the guilty themfelves do not choofe to
cherifh their recollection, and by ruminating
their offences, nourifh themfelves through the
example of their paft, to the perpetration of
future crimes. It is in the relaxation of fecurity,
it is in the expanfion of profperity, it is in the
hour of dilatation of the heart, and of its foften-
ing into feftivity and pleafure, that the real
character of men is difcerned. If there is any
good in them, it appears then or never. Even
wolves and tygers, when gorged with their prey,
are fafe and gentle. It is at fuch times that
noble minds give all the reins to their good-na-
ture. They indulge their genius even to intemperance, in kindnefs to the afflicted, in generofity
to the conquered; forbearing infults, forgiving
injuries, overpaying benefits. Full of dignity
themfelves, they refpect dignity in all, but they
feel it facred in the unhappy. But it is then, and

bafking

bafking in the funfhine of unmerited fortune, that low, fordid, ungenerous, and reptile fouls fwell with their hoarded poifons; it is then that they difplay their odious fplendor, and fhine out in the full luftre of their native villainy and bafe-nefs. It is in that feafon that no man of fenfe or honour can be miftaken for one of them. It was in fuch a feafon, for them of political eafe and fecurity, tho' their people were but juft emerged from actual famine, and were ready to be plunged into a gulph of penury and beggary, that your philofophic lords chofe, with an oftentatious pomp and luxury, to feaft an in-credible number of idle and thoughtlefs people collected with art and pains, from all quarters of the world. They conftructed a vaft amphi-theatre in which they raifed a fpecies of* pillory. On this pillory they fet their lawful king and queen, with an infulting figure over their heads. There they expofed thefe objects of pity and re-fpect to all good minds, to the derifion of an unthinking and unprincipled multitude, dege-nerated even from the verfatile tendernefs which marks the irregular and capricious feelings of the populace. That their cruel infult might have

* The pillory (carcan) in England is generally made very high, like that raifed for expofing the King of France.

7

nothing

nothing wanting to complete it, they chofe the anniverfary of that day in which they expofed the life of their prince to the moft imminent dangers, and the vileft indignities, juft following the inftant when the affaffins, whom they had hired without owning, firft openly took up arms againft their king, corrupted his guards, furprized his caftle, butchered fome of the poor invalids of his garrifon, murdered his governor, and, like wild beafts, tore to pieces the chief magiftrate of his capital city, on account of his fidelity to his fervice.

Till the juftice of the world is awakened, fuch as thefe will go on, without admonition, and without provocation, to every extremity. Thofe who have made the exhibition of the 14th of July, are capable of every evil. They do not commit crimes for their defigns ; but they form defigns that they may commit crimes. It is not their neceffity, but their nature, that impels them. They are modern philofophers, which when you fay of them, you exprefs every thing that is ignoble, favage, and hard-hearted.

Befides the fure tokens which are given by the fpirit of their particular arrangements, there are fome characteriftic lineaments in the general policy of your tumultuous defpotifm,

tifm, which, in my opinion, indicate beyond a
doubt that no revolution whatfoever *in their difpofition* is to be expected. I mean their fcheme of
educating the rifing generation, the principles
which they intend to inftil, and the fympathies
which they wifh to form in the mind, at the
feafon in which it is the moft fufceptible. Inftead of forming their young minds to that do-
cility, to that modefty, which are the grace and
charm of youth, to an admiration of famous ex-
amples, and to an averfenefs to any thing which
approaches to pride, petulance, and felf-conceit,
(diftempers to which that time of life is of itfelf fufficiently liable) they artificially foment
thefe evil difpofitions, and even form them into
fprings of action. Nothing ought to be more
weighed than the nature of books recommended
by public authority. So recommended, they
foon form the character of the age. Uncertain
indeed is the efficacy, limited indeed is the extent of a virtuous inftitution. But if education
takes in *vice* as any part of its fyftem, there is
no doubt but that it will operate with abundant
energy, and to an extent indefinite. The magiftrate, who in favour of freedom thinks himfelf obliged to fuffer all forts of publications, is
under a ftricter duty than any other, well to

confider

confider what fort of writers he fhall authorize.; and fhall recommend, by the ftrongeft of all fanctions, that is, by public honours and rewards. He ought to be cautious how he recommends authors of mixed or ambiguous morality. He ought to be fearful of putting into the hands of youth · writers indulgent to the peculiarities of their own complexion, left they fhould teach the humours of the profeffor, rather than the principles of the fcience. He ought, above all, to be cautious in recommending any writer who has carried marks of a deranged underftanding; for where there is no found reafon, there can be no real virtue; and madnefs is ever vitious and malignant.

The National Affembly proceeds on maxims the very reverfe of thefe. The Affembly recommends to its youth a ftudy of the bold experimenters in morality. Every body knows that there is a great difpute amongft their leaders, which of them is the beft refemblance to Rouffeau. In truth, they all refemble him. His blood they transfufe into their minds and into their manners. Him they ftudy; him they meditate; him they turn over in all the time they can fpare from the laborious mifchief of the day, or the debauches of the night. Rouffeau is their canon of

3   holy

holy writ ; in his life he is their canon of *Polycle-tus* ; he is their ftandard figure of perfection. To this man and this writer, as a pattern to authors and to Frenchmen, the founderies of Paris are now running for ftatues, with the kettles of their poor and the bells of their churches. If an author had written like a great genius on geometry, though his practical and fpeculative morals were vitious in the extreme, it might appear that in voting the ftatue, they honoured only the geometrician. But Roufleau is a moralift, or he is nothing. It is impoffible, therefore, putting the circumftances together, to miftake their defign in choofing the author, with whom they have begun to recommend a courfe of ftudies.

Their great problem is to find a fubftitute for all the principles which hitherto have been employed to regulate the human will and action. They find difpofitions in the mind, of fuch force and quality, as may fit men, far better than the old morality, for the purpofes of fuch a ftate as theirs, and may go much further in fupporting their power, and deftroying their enemies. They have therefore chofen a felfifh, flattering, feductive, oftentatious vice, in the place of plain duty. True humility, the bafis of the Chriftian
fyftem,

fyftem, is the low, but deep and firm foundation of all real virtue. But this, as very pain-
ful in the practice, and little impofing in the
appearance, they have totally difcarded. Their
object is to merge all natural and all focial fentiment in inordinate vanity. In a fmall degree,
and converfant in little things, vanity is of little
moment. When full grown, it is the worft of
vices, and the occafional mimick of them all.
It makes the whole man falfe. It leaves nothing fincere or truft-worthy about him. His
beft qualities are poifoned and perverted by it,
and operate exactly as the worft. When your
lords had many writers as immoral as the object of their ftatue (fuch as Voltaire and others)
they chofe Rouffeau; becaufe in him that pecu-
liar vice which they wifhed to erect into a ruling
virtue, was by far the moft confpicuous.

We have had the great profeffor and founder
of *the philofophy of vanity* in England. As I had
good opportunities of knowing his proceedings
almoft from day to day, he left no doubt in my
mind, that he entertained no principle either to
influence his heart, or to guide his underftanding, but *vanity*. With this vice he was poffeffed
to a degree little fhort of madnefs. It is from
the fame deranged eccentric vanity, that this, the

D   infane

infane *Socrates* of the National Affembly, was
impelled to publifh a mad Confeffion of his mad
faults, and to attempt a new fort of glory, from
bringing hardily to light the obfcure and vulgar
vices which we know may fometimes be blended
with eminent talents. He has not obferved on
the nature of vanity, who does not know
that it is omnivorous; that it has no choice in
its food; that it is fond to talk even of its own
faults and vices, as what will excite furprize and
draw attention, and what will pafs at worft for
opennefs and candour. It was this abufe and per-
verfion, which vanity makes even of hypocrify,
which has driven Rouffeau to record a life not
fo much as chequered, or fpotted here and there,
with virtues, or even diftinguifhed by a fingle
good action. It is fuch a life he choofes to
offer to the attention of mankind. It is fuch a
life, that with a wild defiance, he flings in the
face of his Creator, whom he acknowledges
only to brave. Your Affembly, knowing how
much more powerful example is found than
precept, has chofen this man (by his own account without a fingle virtue) for a model. To
him they erect their firft ftatue. From him
they commence their feries of honours and dif-
tinctions.

-It is that new-invented virtue which your
                                        mafters

masters canonize, that led their moral hero con-
stantly to exhaust the stores of his powerful
rhetoric in the expreſſion of univerſal benevolence; whilſt his heart was incapable of har-
bouring one ſpark of common parental affection.
Benevolence to the whole ſpecies, and want of
feeling for every individual with whom the
profeſſors come in contact, form the character of
the new philoſophy. Setting up for an unſocial
independence, this their hero of vanity refuſes
the juſt price of common labour, as well as the
tribute which opulence owes to genius, and
which, when paid, honours the giver and the
receiver; and then he pleads his beggary as an
excuſe for his crimes. He melts with tender-
neſs for thoſe only who touch him by the re-
moteſt relation, and then, without one natural
pang, caſts away, as a ſort of offal and excre-
ment, the ſpawn of his diſguſtful amours, and
ſends his children to the hoſpital of foundlings.
The bear loves, licks, and forms her young; but
bears are not philoſophers. Vanity, however,
finds its account in reverſing the train of our natural feelings. Thouſands admire the ſentimental
writer; the affectionate father is hardly known
in his pariſh.

Under this philoſophic inſtructor in the *ethics*

of

of vanity, they have attempted in France a re-
generation of the moral conftitution of man.
Statefmen, like your prefent rulers, exift by
every thing which is fpurious, fictitious, and falfe;
by every thing which takes the man from his
houfe, and fets him on a ftage, which makes him
up an artificial creature, with painted theatric
fentiments, fit to be feen by the glare of candle-
light, and formed to be contemplated at a due
diftance. Vanity is too apt to prevail in all of
us, and in all countries. To the improvement
of Frenchmen it feems not abfolutely neceflary
that it fhould be taught upon fyftem. But it is
plain that the prefent rebellion was its legitimate
offspring, and it is pioufly fed by that rebellion,
with a daily dole.

If the fyftem of inftitution, recommended by
the Affembly, is falfe and theatric, it is becaufe
their fyftem of government is of the fame character. To that, and to that alone, it is ftrictly
conformable. To underftand either, we muft
connect the morals with the politics of the legiflators. Your practical philofophers, fyfte-
matic in every thing, have wifely began at the
fource. As the relation between parents and
children is the firft among the elements of vulgar,

gar, natural morality*, they erect ſtatues to a wild, ferocious, low-minded, hard-hearted father, of fine general feelings; a lover of his kind, but a hater of his kindred. Your maſters reject the duties of this vulgar relation, as contrary to liberty; as not founded in the ſocial compact; and not binding according to the rights of men; becauſe the relation is not, of courſe, the reſult of *free election*; never ſo on the ſide of the children, not always on the part of the parents.

The next relation which they regenerate by their ſtatues to Rouſſeau, is that which is next in ſanctity to that of a father. They differ from thoſe old-faſhioned thinkers, who conſidered pedagogues as ſober and venerable characters, and allied to the parental. The moraliſts of the dark times, *preceptorem ſancti voluere parentis eſſe loco.* In this age of light, they teach the people, that preceptors ought to be in the place of gallants. They ſyſtematically corrupt a very corruptible race, (for ſome time a growing nuiſance amongſt you) a ſet of pert, petulant,

* Filiola' tua te delectari lætor et probari tibi ϝοϝγὲν φυσιϰϝὶ eſſe τ᾽ πϝος τὰ τιϰϝα: etenim, ſi hæc non éſt, nulla poteſt homini eſſe ad hominem naturæ adjunctio: qua ſublata vitæ ſocietas tolletur. Valete Patron [Rouſſeau] et tui condiſcipuli! [L'Aſſemblée Nationale].

Cic. Ep. ad Atticum.

literators,

·literators, to whom, inftead of their proper, but fe-
vere, unoftentatious duties, they affign the brilliant
part of men of wit and pleafure, of gay, young,
military fparks, and danglers at toilets. They
call on the rifing generation in France, to take
a fympathy in the adventures and fortunes, and
they endeavour to engage their fenfibility on
the fide of pedagogues, who betray the moft
awful family trufts, and vitiate their female pu-
pils. They teach the people, that the de-
bauchers of virgins, almoft in the arms of their
parents, may be fafe inmates in their houfe, and
even fit guardians of the honour of thofe hufbands who fucceed legally to the office which
the young literators had pre-occupied, without
afking leave of law or confcience.

Thus they difpofe of all the family relations
of parents and children, hufbands and wives.
Through this fame inftructor, by whom they
corrupt the morals, they corrupt the tafte.
Tafte and elegance, though they are reckoned
only among the fmaller and fecondary morals,
yet are of no mean importance in the regulation
of life. A moral tafte is not of force to turn
vice into virtue; but it recommends virtue with
fomething like the blandifhments of pleafure;
and it infinitely abates the evils of vice.

x   Rouffeau,

Rouſſeau, a writer of great force and vivacity, is totally deſtitute of taſte in any ſenſe of the word. Your maſters, who are his ſcholars, conceive that all refinement has an ariſtocratic cha-·racter. The laſt age had exhauſted all its powers in giving a grace and nobleneſs to our natural appetites, and in raiſing them into higher claſs and order than ſeemed juſtly to belong to them. Through Rouſſeau, your maſters are reſolved to deſtroy theſe ariſtocratic prejudices. The paſſion called love, has ſo general and powerful an influence; it makes ſo much of the entertainment, and indeed ſo much the occupation of that part of life which decides the character for ever, that the mode and the principles on which it engages the ſympathy, and ſtrikes the imagination, become of the utmoſt importance to the morals and manners of every ſociety. Your rulers were well aware of this; and in their ſyſtem of changing your manners to accommodate them to their politics, they found nothing ſo convenient as Rouſſeau. Through him they teach men to love after the faſhion of philoſophers; that is, they teach to men, to Frenchmen, a love without gallantry; a love without any thing of that fine flower of youthfulneſs and gentility, which places it, if not

among

among the virtues, among the ornaments of life. Inſtead of this paſſion, naturally allied to grace and manners, they infuſe into their youth an unfaſhioned, indelicate, four, gloomy, ferocious medley of pedantry and lewdneſs; of metaphyſical ſpeculations, blended with the coarſeſt ſenſuality. Such is the general morality of the paſſions to be found in their famous philoſopher, in his famous work of philoſophic gallantry, the *Nouvelle Eloiſe.*

When the fence from the gallantry of preceptors is broken down, and your families are no longer protected by decent pride, and ſalutary domeſtic prejudice, there is but one ſtep to a frightful corruption. The rulers in the National Aſſembly are in good hopes that the females of the firſt families in France may become an eaſy prey to dancing-maſters, fidlers, pattern-drawers, friſeurs, and valets de chambre, and other active citizens of that deſcription, who having the entry into your houſes, and being half-domeſticated by their ſituation, may be blended with you by regular and irregular relations. By a law, they have made theſe people your equals. By adopting the ſentiments of Rouſſeau, they have made them your rivals. In this manner, theſe great legiſlators complete their plan of of levelling, and eftablifh their rights of men on a fure foundation.

I am certain that the writings of Rouffeau lead directly to this kind of fhameful evil. I have often wondered how he comes to be fo much more admired and followed on the continent than he is here. Perhaps a fecret charm in the language may have its fhare in this extraordinary difference. We certainly perceive, and to a degree we feel, in this writer, a ftyle glowing, animated, enthufiaftic; at the fame time that we find it lax, diffufe, and not in the beft tafte of compofition; all the members of the piece being pretty equally laboured and expanded, without any due felection or fubordination of parts. He is generally too much on the ftretch, and his manner has little variety. We cannot reft upon any of his works, though they contain obfervations which occafionally difcover a confiderable infight into human nature. But his doctrines, on the whole, are fo inapplicable to real life and manners, that we never dream of drawing from them any rule for laws or conduct, or for fortifying or illuftrating any thing by a reference to his opinions. They have with us the fate of older paradoxes,

Cum ventum ad verum eft fenfus morefque repugnant,
Atque ipfa utilitas jufti prope mater et æqui.

Perhaps

Perhaps bold fpeculations are more acceptable, becaufe more new to you than to us, who have been long fince fatiated with them. We continue, as in the two laft ages, to read more generally, than I believe is now done on the continent, the authors of found antiquity. Thefe occupy our minds. They give us another tafte and turn; and will not fuffer us to be more than tranfiently amufed with paradoxical morality. It is not that I confider this writer as wholly deftitute of juft notions. Amongft his irregularities, it muft be reckoned, that he is fometimes moral, and moral in a very fublime ftrain. But the *general fpirit and tendency* of his works is mifchievous; and the more mifchievous for this mixture: For, perfect depravity of fentiment is not reconcileable with eloquence; and the mind (though corruptible, not complexionally vitious) would reject and throw off with difguft, a leffon of pure and unmixed evil. Thefe writers make even virtue a pander to vice.

However, I lefs confider the author, than the fyftem of the Affembly in perverting morality, through his means. This I confefs makes me nearly defpair of any attempt upon the minds of their followers, through reafon, honour, or confcience. The great object of your tyrants,

is

is to deftroy the gentlemen of France; and for that purpofe they deftroy, to the beft of their power, all the effect of thofe relations which may render confiderable men powerful or even fafe. To deftroy that order, they vitiate the whole community. That no means may exift of confederating againft their tyranny, by the falfe fympathies of this Nouvelle Eloife, they endeavour to fubvert thofe principles of do-meftic truft and fidelity, which form the difcipline of focial life. They propagate principles by which every fervant may think it, if not his duty, at leaft his privilege, to betray his mafter. By thefe principles, every confiderable father of a family lofes the fanctuary of his houfe. *Debet fua cuique domus effe perfugium tu tiffimum*, fays the law, which your legiflators have taken fo much pains firft to decry, then to repeal. They deftroy all the tranquillity and fecurity of domeftic life; turning the afylum of the houfe into a gloomy prifon, where the father of the family muft drag out a miferable exiftence, endangered in proportion to the apparent means of his fafety; where he is worfe than folitary in a croud of domeftics, and more apprehenfive from his fervants and inmates, than from the hired blood-
thirfty

thirfty mob without doors, who are ready to
pull him to the lanterne.

It is thus, and for the fame end, that they
endeavour to deftroy that tribunal of confcience
which exifts independently of edicts and decrees.
Your defpots govern by terror. They know,
that he who fears God fears nothing elfe; and
therefore they eradicate from the mind, through
their Voltaire, their Helvetius, and the reft of
that infamous gang, that only fort of fear which
generates true courage. Their object is, that
their fellow citizens may be under the dominion
of no awe, but that of their committee of refearch, and of their lanterne.

Having found the advantage of affaffination
in the formation of their tyranny, it is the grand
refource in which they truft for the fupport of it.
Whoever oppofes any of their proceedings, or is
fufpected of a defign to oppofe them, is to anfwer
it with his life, or the lives of his wife and children. This infamous, cruel, and cowardly practice
of affaffination, they have the impudence to call
merciful. They boaft that they have operated their
ufurpation rather by terror than by force; and
that a few feafonable murders have prevented
the bloodfhed of many battles. There is no
doubt

doubt they will extend thefe acts of mercy when-ever they fee an occafion. Dreadful, however, will be the confequences of their attempt to avoid the evils of war, by the merciful policy of murder. If, by effectual punifhment of the guilty, they do not wholly difavow that practice, and the threat of it too, as any part of their policy; if ever a foreign prince enters into France, he muft enter it as into a country of affaffins. The mode of civilized war will not be practifed: nor are the French who act on the prefent fyftem entitled to expect it. They, whofe known policy it is to affaffinate every citizen whom they fufpect to be difcontented by their tyranny, and to corrupt the foldiery of every open enemy, muft look for no modified hoftility. All war, which is not battle, will be military execution. This will beget acts of retaliation from you; and every retaliation will beget a new revenge. The hell-hounds of war, on all fides, will be uncoupled and unmuzzled. The new fchool of murder and barbarifm, fet up in Paris, having deftroyed (fo far as in it lies) all the other manners and principles which have hitherto civilized Europe, will deftroy alfo the mode of civilized war, which, more than any thing elfe, has diftinguifhed the Chriftian world.

Such

Such is the approaching golden age, which the *Virgil of your Affembly has fung to his Pollios !

In fuch a fituation of your political, your civil, and your focial morals and manners, how can you be hurt by the freedom of any difcuf-fion? Caution is for thofe who have fomething to lofe. What I have faid to juftify myfelf in not apprehending any ill confequence from a free difcuffion of the abfurd confequences which flow from the relation of the lawful King to the ufurped conftitution, will apply to my vindica-tion with regard to the expofure I have made of the ftate of the army under the fame fophiftic ufurpation. The prefent tyrants want no argu-ments to prove, what they muft daily feel, that no good army can exift on their principles. They are in no want of a monitor to fuggeft to them the policy of getting rid of the army, as well as of the King, whenever they are in a condition to effect that meafure. What hopes may be entertained of your army for the reftora-tion of your liberties, I know not. At prefent, yielding obedience to the pretended orders of a King, who, they are perfectly apprifed, has no will, and who never can iffue a mandate, which is not intended, in the firft operation, or

* Mirabeau's fpeech concerning univerfal peace.

in

in its certain confequences, for his own deftruction, your army feems·to make one of the principal links .in the chain of that fervitude of anarchy, by which a cruel ufurpation holds an undone
people at once in bondage and confufion.

You afk me what I think of the conduct of
General Monk. How this affects your cafe, I
cannot tell. I doubt whether you poffefs, in
France, any perfons of a capacity to ferve the.
French monarchy in the fame manner in which
Monk ferved the monarchy of England. The
army which Monk commanded had been formed by Cromwell to a perfection of difcipline
which perhaps has never been exceeded. That
army was befides of an excellent compofition.
The foldiers were men of extraordinary piety
after their mode, of the greateft regularity,
and even feverity of manners; brave in the
field, but modeft, quiet and orderly, in their
quarters ; men who abhorred the idea of affaf-
finating their officers or any other perfons; and
who (they at leaft who ferved in this ifland)
were firmly attached to thofe generals, by
whom they were well treated and ably commanded. Such an army, once gained, might
be depended on. I doubt much, if you could

now

now find a Monk, whether a Monk could find, in France, fuch an army.

I certainly agree with you, that in all probability we owe our whole conftitution to the reftoration of the Englifh monarchy. The ftate of things from which Monk relieved England, was however by no means, at that time, fo deplorable in any fenfe, as yours is now, and under the prefent fway is likely to continue. Cromwell had delivered England from anarchy. His government, though military and defpotic, had been regular and orderly. Under the iron, and under the yoke, the foil yielded its produce. After his death, the evils of anarchy were rather dreaded than felt. Every man was yet fafe in his houfe and in his property. But it muft be admitted, that Monk freed this nation from great and juft apprehenfions both of future anarchy and of probable tyranny in fome form or other. The king whom he gave us was indeed the very reverfe of your benignant fovereign, who in reward for his attempt to beftow liberty on his fubjeéts, languifhes himfelf in prifon. The perfon given to us by Monk was a man without any fenfe of his duty as a prince; without any regard to the dignity of his crown;

without

without any love to his people; diſſolute, falſe, venal, and deſtitute of any poſitive good qua-lity whatſoever, except a pleaſant temper, and the manners of a gentleman. Yet the reſtora-tion of our monarchy, even in the perſon of ſuch a prince, was every thing to us; for without monarchy in England, moſt certainly we never can enjoy either peace or liberty. It was under this conviction that the very firſt regular ſtep which we took on the Revolution of 1688, was to fill the throne with a real king; and even before it could be done in due form, the chiefs of the nation did not attempt themſelves to exer-ciſe authority ſo much as by *interim*. They in-ſtantly requeſted the Prince of Orange to take the government on himſelf. The throne was not effectively vacant for an hour.

Your fundamental laws, as well as ours, ſup-poſe a monarchy. Your zeal, Sir, in ſtanding ſo firmly for it as you have done, ſhews not only a ſacred reſpect for your honour and fidelity, but a well-informed attachment to the real wel-fare and true liberties of your country. I have expreſſed myſelf ill, if I have given you cauſe to imagine, that I prefer the conduct of thoſe who have retired from this warfare to your beha-viour, who, with a courage and conſtancy almoſt

E   ſupernatural,

supernatural, have ftruggled againft tyranny, and
kept the field to the laft. You fee I have corrected the exceptionable part in the edition
which I now fend you. Indeed in fuch terrible
extremities as yours, it is not eafy to fay, in a
political view, what line of conduct is the moft
advifeable. In that ftate of things, I cannot
bring myfelf feverely to condemn perfons who are
wholly unable to bear fo much as the fight of
thofe men in the throne of legiflation, who are
only fit to be the objects of criminal juftice. If
fatigue, if difguft, if unfurmountable naufea,
drive them away from fuch fpectacles, *ubi mife-
riarum pars non mimima erat, videre et afpici,* I
cannot blame them. He muft have an heart of
adamant who could hear a fet of traitors puffed
up with unexpected and undeferved power, obtained by an ignoble, unmanly, and perfidious
rebellion, treating their honeft fellow citizens as
rebels, becaufe they refufed to bind themfelves
through their confcience, againft the dictates of
confcience itfelf, and had declined to fwear an
active compliance with their own ruin. How
could a man of common flefh and blood endure,
that thofe, who but the other day had fkulked
unobferved in their antichambers, fcornfully infulting men, illuftrious in their rank, facred in
their

their function, and venerable in their character, now in decline of life, and fwimming on the wrecks of their fortunes, that thofe mifcreants fhould tell fuch men fcornfully and outrageoufly, after they had robbed them of all their property, that it is more than enough if they are allowed what will keep them from abfolute famine, and that for the reft, they muft let their grey hairs fall over the plough, to make out a fcanty fub-fiftence with the labour of their hands! Laft, and worft, who could endure to hear this un-natural, infolent, and favage defpotifm called liberty? If, at this diftance, fitting quietly by my fire, I cannot read their decrees and fpeeches without indignation, fhall I condemn thofe who have fled from the actual fight and hearing of all thefe horrors? No, no! mankind has no title to demand that we fhould be flaves to their guilt and infolence; or that we fhould ferve them in fpite of themfelves. Minds, fore with the poignant fenfe of infulted virtue, filled with high difdain againft the pride of triumphant bafenefs, often have it not in their choice to ftand their ground. Their complexion (which might defy the rack) cannot go through fuch a trial. Something very high muft fortify men to that proof. But when I am driven to comparifon,

furely

surely I cannot hesitate for a moment to prefer
to such men as are common, those heroes, who
in the midst of despair perform all the tasks of
hope; who subdue their feelings to their duties;
who, in the cause of humanity, liberty, and honour, abandon all the satisfactions of life, and
every day incur a fresh risque of life itself. Do
me the justice to believe that I never can prefer any fastidious virtue (virtue still) to the un-
conquered perseverance, to the affectionate patience of those who watch day and night, by
the bed-side of their delirious country, who,
for their love to that dear and venerable name,
bear all the disgusts, and all the buffets they receive from their frantic mother. Sir, I do look
on you as true martyrs; I regard you as soldiers
who act far more in the spirit of our Comman-
der in chief, and the Captain of our salvation,
than those who have left you; though I must
first bolt myself very thoroughly, and know
that I could do better, before I can censure
them. I assure you, Sir, that, when I consider
your unconquerable fidelity to your sovereign,
and to your country, the courage, fortitude,
magnanimity, and long-suffering of yourself,
and the Abbé Maury, and of Mr. Cazales, and
of many worthy persons of all orders, in your
Assembly,

Aſſembly, I forget, in the luſtre of theſe great qualities, that on your ſide has been diſplayed an eloquence ſo rational, manly, and convincing, that no time or country, perhaps, has ever excelled. But your talents diſappear in my admiration of your virtues.

As to Mr. Mounier and Mr. Lally, I have always wiſhed to do juſtice to their parts, and their eloquence, and the general purity of their motives. Indeed I ſaw very well from the beginning, the miſchiefs which, with all theſe talents and good intentions, they would do to their country, through their confidence in ſyſtems. But their diſtemper was an epidemic malady. They were young and inexperienced; and when will young and inexperienced men learn caution and diſtruſt of themſelves? And when will men, young or old, if ſuddenly raiſed to far higher power than that which abſolute kings and emperors commonly enjoy, learn any thing like moderation? Monarchs in general reſpect ſome ſettled order of things, which they find it difficult to move from its baſis, and to which they are obliged to conform, even when there are no poſitive limitations to their power. Theſe gentlemen conceived that they were choſen to new model the ſtate, and even the whole order of civil ſociety

E 3   itſelf.

itfelf. No wonder that *they* entertained dange-
rous vifions, when the King's minifters, truftees
for the facred depofit of the monarchy, were fo
infected with the contagion of project and fyftem (I can hardly think it black premeditated
treachery) that they publicly advertifed for plans
and fchemes of government, as if they were to
provide for the rebuilding of an hofpital that had
been burned down. What was this, but to un-
chain the fury of rafh fpeculation amongft a
people, of itfelf but too apt to be guided by a
heated imagination, and a wild fpirit of adven-
ture?

The fault of Mr. Mounier and Mr. Lally
was very great; but it was very general. If
thofe gentlemen ftopped when they came to the
brink of the gulph of guilt and public mifery,
that yawned before them in the abyfs of thefe
dark and bottomlefs fpeculations, I forgive their
firft error; in that they were involved with many.
Their repentance was their own.

They who confider Mounier and Lally as de-
ferters, muft regard themfelves as murderers and
as traitors: for from what elfe than murder and
treafon did they defert? For my part, I honour
them for not having carried miftake into crime.
If, indeed, I thought that they were not cured
by

by experience; that they were not made fenfible
that thofe who would reform a ftate, ought to
affume fome actual conftitution of government
which is to be reformed; if they are not at
length fatisfied that it is become a neceffary preli-
minary to liberty in France, to commence by the
re-eftablifhment of order and property of *every*
kind, through the re-eftablifhment of their monarchy, of every one of the old habitual diftinc-
tions and claffes of the ftate; if they do not fee that
thefe claffes are not to be confounded in order to
be afterwards revived and feparated; if they are
not convinced that the fcheme of parochial and
club governments takes up the ftate at the
wrong end, and is a low and fenfelefs contrivance (as making the fole conftitution of a fupreme power) I fhould then allow, that their
early rafhnefs ought to be remembered to the
laft moment of their lives.

You gently reprehend me, becaufe in holding
out the picture of your difaftrous fituation, I
fuggeft no plan for a remedy. Alas! Sir, the
propofition of plans, without an attention to circumftances, is the very caufe of all your mif-
fortunes; and never fhall you find me aggrava-
ting, by the infufion of any fpeculations of mine,
the evils which have arifen from the fpeculations

E 4 of

of others. Your malady, in this respect, is a disorder of repletion. You seem to think, that my keeping back my poor ideas, may arise from an indifference to the welfare of a foreign, and sometimes an hostile nation. No, Sir, I faithfully assure you, my reserve is owing to no such causes. Is this letter, swelled to a second book, a mark of national antipathy, or even of national indifference? I should act altogether in the spirit of the same caution, in a similar state of our own domestic affairs. If I were to venture any advice, in any case, it would be my best. The sacred duty of an adviser (one of the most inviolable that exists) would lead me, towards a real enemy, to act as if my best friend were the party concerned. But I dare not risque a speculation with no better view of your affairs than at present I can command; my caution is not from disregard, but from sollicitude for your welfare. It is suggested solely from my dread of becoming the author of inconsiderate counsel.

It is not, that as this strange series of actions has passed before my eyes, I have not indulged my mind in a great variety of political speculations concerning them. But compelled by no such positive duty as does not permit me to evade an opinion; called upon by no ruling

power,

power, without authority as I am, and without
confidence, I fhould ill anfwer my own ideas of
what would become myfelf, or what would be
ferviceable to others, if I were, as a volunteer,
to obtrude any project of mine upon a nation,
to whofe circumftances I could not be fure it
might be applicable.

Permit me to fay, that if I were as confident,
as I ought to be diffident in my own loofe, general ideas, I never fhould venture to broach
them, if but at twenty leagues diftance from the
centre of your affairs. I muft fee with my own
eyes, I muft, in a manner, touch with my own
hands, not only the fixed, but the momentary
circumftances, before I could venture to fuggeft
any political project whatfoever. I muft know
the power and difpofition to accept, to execute,
to perfevere. I muft fee all the aids, and all the
obftacles. I muft fee the means of correcting
the plan, where correctives would be wanted.
I muft fee the things; I muft fee the men.
Without a concurrence and adaptation of thefe to
the defign, the very beft fpeculative projects might
become not only ufelefs, but mifchievous. Plans
muft be made for men. We cannot think of
making men, and binding nature to our defigns.
People at a diftance muft judge ill of men.
They

They do not always anſwer to their reputation
when you approach them. Nay, the perſpec-
tive varies, and ſhews them quite otherwiſe than
you thought them. At a diſtance, if we judge
uncertainly of men, we muſt judge worſe of
opportunities, which continually vary their ſhapes
and colours, and paſs away like clouds. The
Eaſtern politicians never do any thing without
the opinion of the aſtrologers on the *fortunate
moment.* They are in the right, if they can do
no better; for the opinion of fortune is ſome-
thing towards commanding it. Stateſmen of a
more judicious preſcience, look for the fortunate
moment too; but they ſeek it, not in the conjunctions and oppoſitions of planets, but in the
conjunctions and oppoſitions of men and things.
Theſe form their almanack.

To illuſtrate the miſchief of a wiſe plan, without any attention to means and circumſtances, it
is not neceſſary to go farther than to your recent
hiſtory. In the condition in which France was
found three years ago, what better ſyſtem could
be propoſed, what leſs, even favouring of wild
theory, what fitter to provide for all the exigencies, whilſt it reformed all the abuſes of government, than the convention of the States
General? I think nothing better could be ima-
gined.

5

gined. But I have cenfured, and do ftill pre-
fume to cenfure your Parliament of Paris, for
not having fuggefted to the King, that this proper meafure was of all meafures the moft critical and arduous; one in which the utmoft cir-
cumfpection, and the greateft number of pre-
cautions, were the moft abfolutely neceffary.
The very confeffion that a government wants
either amendment in its conformation, or relief
to great diftrefs, caufes it to lofe half its reputation, and as great a proportion of its ftrength
as depends upon that reputation. It was therefore neceffary, firft to put government out of
danger, whilft at its own defire it fuffered fuch
an operation, as a general reform at the hands of
thofe who were much more filled with a fenfe of
the difeafe, than provided with rational means of
a cure.

It may be faid, that this care, and thefe pre-
cautions, were more naturally the duty of the
King's minifters, than that of the Parliament.
They were fo; but every man muft anfwer in his
eftimation for the advice he gives, when he puts
the conduct of his meafure into hands who he
does not know will execute his plans according
to his ideas. Three or four minifters were not
to be trufted with the being of the French monarchy,

narchy, of all the orders, and of all the dif-
tinctions, and all the property of the kingdom.
What muft be the prudence of thofe who could
think, in the then known temper of the people
of Paris, of affembling the ftates at a place
fituated as Verfailles?

.. The Parliament of Paris did worfe than to
infpire this blind confidence into the King. For,
as if names were things, they took no notice of
(indeed they rather countenanced) the deviations
which were manifeft in the execution, from the
true antient principles of the plan which they
recommended. Thefe deviations (as guardians
of the antient laws, ufages, and conftitution of
the kingdom) the Parliament of Paris ought
not to have fuffered, without the ftrongeft re-
monftrances to the throne. It ought to have
founded the alarm to the whole nation, as it had
often done on things of infinitely lefs importance.
Under pretence of refufcitating the antient conftitution, the Parliament faw one of the ftrongeft
acts of innovation, and the moft leading in its
confequences, carried into effect before their
eyes; and an innovation through the medium of
defpotifm; that is, they fuffered the King's minifters to new model the whole reprefentation of
the *Tiers Etat*, and, in a great meafure, that of the

clergy

clergy too, and to deſtroy the antient propor-
tions of the orders. Theſe changes, unqueſ-
tionably the King had no right to make; and
here the Parliaments failed in their duty, and
along with their country, have periſhed by this
failure.

What a number of faults have led to this
multitude of misfortunes, and almoſt all from
this one ſource, that of conſidering certain general maxims, without attending to circumſtances, to times, to places, to conjunctures,
and to actors! If we do not attend ſcrupulouſly
to all theſe, the medicine of to-day becomes the
poiſon of to-morrow. If any meaſure was in
the abſtract better than another, it was to call
the ſtates—*ea viſa ſalus morientibus una.*—Certainly it had the appearance.—But ſee the conſe-
quences of not attending to critical moments,
of not regarding the ſymptoms which diſcrimi-
nate diſeaſes, and which diſtinguiſh conſtitutions,
complexions, and humours.

—— Mox fuerat hoc ipſum exitio; furiiſque refecti,
Ardebant; ipſique ſuos, jam morte ſub ægra,
Diſciſſos nudis laniabant dentibus artus.

Thus the potion which was given to ſtrengthen
the conſtitution, to heal diviſions, and to com-
poſe

poſe the minds of men, became the ſource of debility, phrenzy, diſcord, and utter diſſolution.

In this, perhaps, I have anſwered, I think, another of your queſtions—Whether the Britiſh conſtitution is adapted to your circumſtances? When I praiſed the Britiſh conſtitution, and wiſhed it to be well ſtudied, I did not mean that its exterior form and poſitive arrangement ſhould become a model for you, or for any people ſervilely to copy. I meant to recommend the *principles* from which it has grown, and the policy on which it has been progreſſively improved out of elements common to you and to us. I am ſure it is no viſionary theory of mine. It is not an advice that ſubjects you to the hazard of any experiment. I believed the antient principles to be wiſe in all caſes of a large empire that would be free. I thought you poſſeſſed our principles in your old forms, in as great a perfection as we did originally. If your ſtates agreed (as I think they did) with your circumſtances, they were beſt for you. As you had a conſtitution formed upon principles ſimilar to ours, my idea was, that you might have improved them as we have done, conforming them to the ſtate and exigencies of the times,

and

and the condition of property in your country, having the confervation of that property, and the fubftantial bafis of your' monarchy, as principal objects in all your reforms.

I do not advife an Houfe of Lords to you. Your antient courfe by reprefentatives of the Nobleffe (in your circumftances) appears to me rather a better inftitution. I know, that with you, a fet of men of rank have betrayed their conftituents, their honour, their truft, their King, and their country, and levelled themfelves with their footmen, that through this degradation they might afterwards put themfelves above their natural equals. Some of thefe perfons have entertained a project, that in reward of this their black perfidy and corruption, they may be chofen to give rife to a new order, and to eftablifh themfelves into an Houfe of Lords. Do you think that, under the name of a Britifh conftitution, I mean to recommend to you fuch Lords, made of fuch kind of ftuff? I do not however include in this defcription all of thofe who are fond of this fcheme.

If you were now to form fuch an Houfe of Peers, it would bear, in my opinion, but little refemblance to our's in its origin, character, or the purpofes which it might anfwer, at the fame time

time that it would deftroy your true natural no-
bility. But if you are not in a condition to
frame an Houfe of Lords, ftill lefs are you capable, in my opinion, of framing any thing
which virtually and fubftantially could be an-
fwerable (for the purpofes of a ftable, regular
government) to our Houfe of Commons. That
Houfe is, within itfelf, a much more fubtle and
artificial combination of parts and powers, than
people are generally aware of. What knits it to
the other members of the conftitution; what fits it
to be at once the great fupport, and the great con-
troul of government; what makes it of fuch
admirable fervice to that monarchy which, if it
limits, it fecures and ftrengthens, would require
a long difcourfe, belonging to the leifure of a
contemplative man, not to one whofe duty it is
to join in communicating praɗically to the people
the bleffings of fuch a conftitution.

Your *Tiers Etat* was not in effeɗ and fub-
ftance an Houfe of Commons. You ftood in abfolute need of fomething elfe to fupply the manifeft
defeɗs in fuch a body as your Tiers Etat. On a fober
and difpaffionate view of your old conftitution, as
conneɗed with all the prefent circumftances, I
was fully perfuaded, that the crown, ftanding as
things have ftood (and are likely to ftand, if you

are

are to have any monarchy at all) was and is incapable, alone and by itſelf, of holding a juſt balance
between the two orders, and at the ſame time of
effecting the interior and exterior purpoſes of a
protecting government. I, whoſe leading principle it is, in a reformation of the ſtate, to make uſe
of exiſting materials, am of opinion, that the re-
preſentation of the clergy, as a ſeparate order,
was an inſtitution which touched all the orders
more nearly than any of them touched the other;
that it was well fitted to connect them; and to
hold a place in any wiſe monarchical commonwealth. If I refer you to your original conſtitution, and think it, as I do, ſubſtantially a good
one, I do not amuſe you in this, more than in
other things, with any inventions of mine. A
certain intemperance of intellect is the diſeaſe
of the time, and the ſource of all its other diſeaſes. I will keep myſelf as untainted by it as
I can. Your architects build without a foundation. I would readily lend an helping hand to
any ſuperſtructure, when once this is effectually
ſecured—but firſt I would ſay δος πν ϛω.

You think, Sir, and you may think rightly, upon
the firſt view of the theory, that to provide for the
exigencies of an empire, ſo ſituated and ſo related
as that of France, its King ought to be inveſted

F   with

with powers very much superior to those which
the King of England possesses under the letter of
our constitution. Every degree of power ne-
cessary to the state, and not destructive to the
rational and moral freedom of individuals, to
that personal liberty, and personal security,
which contribute so much to the vigour, the
prosperity, the happiness, and the dignity of a
nation—every degree of power which does not
suppose the total absence of all control, and all
responsibility on the part of ministers,—a King of
France, in common sense, ought to possess. But
whether the exact measure of authority, assigned
by the letter of the law to the King of Great
Britain, can answer to the exterior or interior
purposes of the French monarchy, is a point
which I cannot venture to judge upon. Here,
both in the power given, and its limitations, we
have always cautiously felt our way. The parts
of our constitution have gradually, and almost
insensibly, in a long course of time, accommodated
themselves to each other, and to their common,
as well as to their separate purposes. But this
adaptation of contending parts, as it has not been
in our's, so it can never be in your's, or in any
country, the effect of a single instantaneous regulation, and no sound heads could ever think of
doing it in that manner.

I believe,

I, believe, Sir, that many on the continent altogether miſtake the condition of a King of Great Britain. He is a real King, and not an executive officer. If he will not trouble himſelf with contemptible details, nor wiſh to degrade himſelf by becoming a party in little ſquabbles, I am far from ſure, that a King of Great Britain, in whatever concerns him as a King, or indeed as a rational man, who combines his public intereſt with his perſonal ſatisfaction, does not poſſeſs a more real, ſolid, extenſive power, than the King of France was poſſeſſed of before this miſerable Revolution. The direct power of the King of England is conſiderable. His indirect, and far more certain power, is great indeed. He ſtands in need of nothing towards dignity; of nothing towards ſplendour; of nothing towards authority; of nothing at all towards conſideration abroad. When was it that a King of England wanted wherewithal to make him reſpected, courted, or perhaps even feared in every ſtate in Europe?

I am conſtantly of opinion, that your ſtates, in three orders, on the footing on which they ſtood in 1614, were capable of being brought into a proper and harmonious combination with royal authority. This conſtitution by eſtates,

was

was the natural, and only juft reprefentation of France. It grew out of the habitual condi-. tions, relations, and reciprocal claims of men. It grew out of the circumftances of the country, and out of the ftate of property. The wretched fcheme of your prefent mafters, is not to fit the conftitution to the people, but wholly to deftroy conditions, to diffolve relations, to change the ftate of the nation, and to fubvert property, in order to fit their country to their theory of a conftitution.

Until you could make out pra'ically that great work, a combination of oppofing forces, " a work of labour long, and endlefs praife," the utmoft caution ought to have been ufed in the reduction of the royal power, which alone was capable of holding togetlier the comparatively heterogeneous mafs of your ftates. But at this day, all thefe confiderations are unfeafonable. To what end fhould we difcufs the limitations of royal power? Your king is in prifon. Why fpeculate òn the meafure and ftandard of liber-ty? I doubt much, very much indeed, whether France is at all ripe for liberty on any ftandard. Men are qualified for civil liberty, in exact pro-portion to their difpofition to put moral chains upon their own appetites; in proportion as their

§   love

love to juftice is above their rapacity; in proportion as their foundnefs and fobriety of underftanding is above their vanity and prefumption;
in proportion as they are more difpofed to liften
to the counfels of the wife and good, in pre-
ference to the flattery of knaves. Society cannot exift unlefs a controlling power upon will
and appetite be placed fomewhere, and the lefs
of it there is within, the more there muft be
without. It is ordained in the eternal conftitution of things, that men of intemperate
minds cannot be free. Their paffions forge
their fetters.

This fentence the prevalent part of your
countrymen execute on themfelves. They poffeffed, not long fince, what was next to freedom, a mild paternal monarchy. They defpifed
it for its weaknefs. They were offered a well-
poifed free conftitution. It did not fuit their
tafte or their temper. They carved for themfelves; they flew out, murdered, robbed, and
rebelled. They have fucceeded, and put over
their country an infolent tyranny, made up of
cruel and inexorable mafters, and that too of a
defcription hitherto not known in the world.
The powers and policies by which they have
fucceeded, are not thofe of great ftatefmen, or

F 3   great

great military commanders, but the practices of incendiaries, affassins, housebreakers,. robbers, spreaders of false news, forgers of false orders from authority, and other delinquencies, of which ordinary justice takes cognizance. Accordingly the spirit of their rule is exactly correspondent to the means by which they obtained it. They act more in the manner of thieves who have got possession of an house, than of conquerors who have subdued a nation.

Opposed to these, in appearance, but in appearance only, is another band, who call themselves the *moderate*. These, if I conceive rightly of their conduct, are a set of men who approve heartily of the whole new constitution, but wish to lay heavy on the most atrocious of those crimes, by which this fine constitution of their's has been obtained. They are a sort of people who affect to proceed as if they thought that men may deceive without fraud, rob without injustice, and overturn every thing without violence. They are men who would usurp the government of their country with decency and moderation. In fact they are nothing more or better, than men engaged in desperate designs, with feeble minds. They are not honest; they are only ineffectual and unsystematic in their iniquity.

iniquity. They are perfons who want not the difpofitions, but the energy and vigour, that is neceſſary for great evil machinations. · They find that in fuch defigns they fall at beft into a fecondary rank, and others take the place and lead in ufurpation, which they are not qualified to obtain or to hold. They envy to their companions, the natural fruit of their crimes; they join to run them down with the hue and cry of mankind, which purfues their common offences; and then hope to mount into their places on the credit of the fobriety with which they fhew themfelves difpofed to carry on what may feem moft plaufible in the mifchievous projeƈts they purfue in common. But thefe men naturally are defpifed by thofe who have heads to know, and hearts that are able to go through the neceſſary demands of bold, wicked enterprizes. They are naturally claſſed below the latter defcription, and will only be ufed by them as inferior inftruments. They will be only the Fairfaxes of your Crom-wells. If they mean honeftly, why do they not ftrengthen the arms of honeft men, to fupport their antient, legal, wife, and free government, given to them in the fpring of 1788, againft the inventions of craft, and the theories of igno-rance and folly ? If they do not, they muft con-

tinue

tinue the fcorn of both parties; fometimes the
tool, fometimes the incumbrance of that, whofe
views they approve, whofe conduct they decry. Thefe people are only made to be the
fport of tyrants. They never can obtain, or
communicate freedom.

You afk me too, whether we have a committee of refearch. No, Sir,—God forbid! It is
the neceffary inftrument of tyranny and ufurpation; and therefore I do not wonder that it has
had an early eftablifhment under your prefent
Lords. We do not want it.

Excufe my length. I have been fomewhat
occupied, fince I was honoured with your letter;
and I fhould not have been able to anfwer it at
all, but for the holidays, which have given me
means of enjoying the leifure of the country.
I am called to duties which I am neither able
nor willing to evade. I muft foon return to
my old conflict with the corruptions and op-
preffions which have prevailed in our eaftern
dominions. I muft turn myfelf wholly from
thofe of France.

In England, we *cannot* work fo hard as Frenchmen. Frequent relaxation is neceffary to us.
You are naturally more intenfe in your applica-
tion. I did not know this part of your national
character,

character, until I went into France in 1773. At present, this your difpofition to labour is rather encreafed than leffened. In your Affembly you do not allow yourfelves a recefs even on Sundays. We have two days in the week, befides the feftivals; and befides five or fix months of the fummer and autumn. This continued unremitted effort of the members of your Affembly, I take to be one among the caufes of the mifchief they have done. They who always labour, can have no true judgment. You never give yourfelves time to cool. You can never furvey, from its proper point of fight, the work you have finifhed, before you decree its final execution. You can never plan the future by the paft. You never go into the country, foberly and difpaffionately to obferve the effect of your meafures on their objects. You cannot feel diftinctly how far the people are rendered better and improved, or more miferable and depraved, by what you have done. You cannot fee with your own eyes the fufferings and afflictions you caufe. You know them but at a diftance, on the ftatements of thofe who always flatter the reigning power, and who, amidft their reprefentations of the grievances, inflame your

minds

minds againſt thoſe who are oppreſſed. Theſe are
amongſt the effects of unremitted labour, when
men exhauſt their attention, burn out their can-
dles, and are left in the dark.—*Malo meorum
negligentiam, quam iſtorum obſcuram diligentiam.*

Beaconsfield,
January 19th 1791.

I have the honor, &c.

(Signed) *EDMUND BURKE.*

www.ingramcontent.com/pod-product-compliance
Lightning Source LLC
Chambersburg PA
CBHW030009030726
47499CB00008B/2965